seven miles from sydney **manly** a thousand miles from care

Published by David Hancock Photography
PO Box 341
Balgowlah NSW 2093
Australia
Tel: +61 2 9949 6839
Mobile: 0419 692 155
www.davidhancock.com.au

Design & production: Vanessa Wilton (Billy Boy Design)

National Library of Australia Cataloguing-in-Publication

ISBN 978-0-646-48818-9
Printed by Kyodo Printing Co (Singapore) Pte Ltd

Cover: First light, Fairy Bower.

In a continuum as old as
Gondwana itself a massive
winter Sou' Easterly swell
crashes towards the coast at
Freshwater......only a few are
game for the challenge!

manly

Manly, the name always inspires different meanings for different people. I really discovered what it meant for me 25 years ago as I paddled down the harbour in my canoe. A broken relationship caused me that day to move from Rushcutters bay, a place I found over-crowded, to Manly. It was a beautiful day and after crossing the harbour to Bradleys Head we hugged the western side of the harbour as we passed a string of isolated bays and beaches crossing the entrance to Middle Harbour past Crater Cove and on into Manly. I felt I had started a new life.

I have lived nearby the township in the ensuing 25 years enjoying the amazing outdoor environment and the people who inhabit the lower peninsula ever since. I have roamed the hills and headlands overlooking Manly and swum and fished the waters in all weathers. I have closely watched development and change to the environment. The town has always catered to the casual visitor. On a hot summers day the ferries disgorge thousands of visitors from the city and places west. They come for a day in the sun, a swim a coffee an ice cream or a meal. It is a paradise that lodges firmly in the memory for some.

I have soaked up the area in all moods and weathers and my memories are for the most part overwhelmingly positive. As a photographer I am primarily motivated by light. I love the soft warm filtered light reflecting off land, people and architecture. Light is what it is all about for me. If you have never sat at South Steyne as the setting sun filters through the big Norfolk pines and the seas spume illuminating the last of the days activities then you haven't lived. Equally in the morning especially after a big south easterly swell the shapes of people taking their ease and their exercise on the beach as the sun rises over Fairy Bower headland. Or swimming the crystal waters of Fairy Bower at full tide when the wind is from the south eating a simple picnic and then communing beneath the water with the fish of all sizes. Or snorkeling out over the reef out on the Bower, exploring the Aboriginal rock carvings on the magnificent Manly to Spit walk or up on the Wakehurst Parkway and wondering about their lives.

Introduction

North Head is still an absolute treasure, a walk from Fairy Bower up the headland traverses a bewildering variety of three dimensional geography, seascapes and plant and animal life. The absolute integrity of the plant life up there is astounding, with very little exotic interference and the silence one normally only finds in outback Australia. Go up any day and you'll still find a spot where you can find peace and solace.

I'm not sure whether the people who live here appreciate just how beautiful the area is, we tend to get complacent about such things only appreciating the light, the people and the landscape when we return from somewhere else or at special times. As we swig on a can of beer on the Friday 6.30 ferry from Circular Quay or watch the sun set over North Harbour eating a meal on the wharf but I have had a love affair with the place and my hope is that this collection of photographs conveys in some way the intensity of that passion.

contents

David Hancock is a professional freelance photographer based in Manly. David is a photojournalist with over 30 years' experience in national and international media. He has worked with newspapers and magazines in New Zealand and Australia, including the NZ Herald, The Australian, the Sydney Morning Herald, The Australian Women's Weekly and The Bulletin.

For the past ten years he has worked as a freelance photographer. Most of this work has been with corporate clients and international publications such as Hello Magazine in the UK, The London Daily Telegraph and the news agency Agence France Presse.

Coming with a strong background in photojournalism he has an easy rapport with all his subjects and specialises in corporate and location portraiture, industrial photography and all types of reportage and editorial disciplines.

Previous Page: Norfolk Pine, Queenscliff.
Opposite page: Secluded Delwood Beach.

Introduction	5
landscapes	8
beach culture	28
activities	44
community	68
history	90
lifestyle	102

"We got into Port Jackson early in the afternoon, and had the satisfaction of finding the finest harbour in the world, in which a thousand sail of the line may ride in the most perfect security."

Captain Arthur Phillip January 25th 1788

Above: North Harbour Marina.
Opposite page: Sydney Harbour from Dobroyd National Park.

landscapes

Above & opposite: White man's dreaming Crater Cove, Sydney Harbour National Park. The huts were built by returning service-men after the war who wanted a place to rediscover themselves, to fish, to swim and dream a new life. We owe its continued existence to a couple of hard-working descendants who knew it was precious and delicate and have worked hard to maintain it.

Left: Water Dragon at Crater Cove.
Above: Rainbow Lorikeet, Dobroyd Point.
Right: Flannel Flower, Dobroyd Head.
Far right: Cliffs off North Head, Sydney Harbour.

Above: Twilight, Manly Pier walkway.
Opposite page: Winter evening, Manly Cove.

landscapes

Above left: Crow and Bottlebrush, Manly Dam.

Above right: Australian Christmas Bush.

Opposite page: King Parrot.

Above left: Angophora trees, Reef Beach, Sydney Harbour National Park.
Above right: Australian Flannel Flower after bush fire.
Opposite page: Love message, North Head.

Above: A Little Penguin at Reef Beach, Sydney Harbour.
Opposite page: Reef Beach, Sydney Harbour National Park.

Left: Reef Beach, Sydney Harbour National Park.

Above: Little Penguin, Reef Beach, Sydney Harbour National Park. The Little Penguin colony in Manly is now reduced to sixty breeding pairs and considered endangered.

Opposite page: Old time launch owners at Reef Beach.

Left: Forty Baskets Beach, Manly to Spit walk, Sydney Harbour National Park.
Above: Kookaburra, Manly Dam.

Above: Cliffs off North Head National Park.

Right: Sydney Heads from Fairlight Beach.

Left: Boat dog, Manly Cove.

Above: As good as it gets. South Steyne Beach, no wind, no surf, crystal clear water.

Opposite page: Manly Beach, summer during the week.

In the short space of a century Australians have developed their own unique beach culture. In 1902 a few brave souls broke the law to bathe at Manly in daylight hours. The morals and sensibilities of Victorian England were swept away as men and women took to the surf.

The heart of it is a peculiarly Australian worship of ocean and its environs, a living and evolving doctrine seen best expressed in the morning.........

You see it in their open, cheery faces, ready with a joke or a quick retort and a self-deprecating remark. It's a distinctly Australian style born more likely of the coast than of the harsh interior. Whether you like it or not they know they live in the best part of the world. Yes, there's a smug-ness about it sometimes but the best of them are good-hearted souls just looking forward to another relaxed day on the Australian East Coast.

Right: Early morning exercise at South Steyne.

beach culture

Opposite page: Summer promenade.

Above: Local swim club on a stormy winter's morning.

Opposite page: Storm clouds, Manly Beach.

Above: Rush hour in the surf.

Above: The 'Old and the Bold', South Steyne.
Opposite page: Surfboat training, North Harbour.

beach culture

Opposite page: First light, Fairy Bower.

Above: A steep break at Deadman's.

beach culture

Opposite page: Charlotte Boney from Brewarrina on her first day at the beach.

Above: Young couple, strong current, South Steyne.

Right: Dawn exercise, South Steyne Beach.

Above: School sport, surf paddling.

beach culture

Above: Child play, Shelly Beach.

Above right: Teenage girls, South Steyne Beach.

Far right: Sunset silhouette.

Right: Surfers, Queenscliff.

Geography dictates what you can do in Manly. The options for the creative outdoor person are endless. If the wind is blowing onshore at Ocean beach then Manly cove, Collins Flat and Delwood beaches are an easy walk. Likewise if there's a cold southerly Fairy Bower is perfectly protected. Yes, there are endless cafes in which to linger but if you've got a fit body and a creative mind the opportunities are endless.

Right: Teenagers at Jump Rock, Collins Flat.

activities

Left: Historic 18 footer racing yacht, Manly Cove.

Right: Coffee at Manly Wharf.

Opposite page: Fairy Bower on a late autumn morning.

Opposite & above: The annual Wine and Food Festival.....music, colour, laughter and dance if you feel inclined.

Above: The Manly Jazz Festival.

Right & opposite page: Manly Markets

Above: Morning coffee at The Bower.

Opposite page: Teen girls hang out and swim at Manly wharf.

activities

Opposite page: Fairy Bower pool, Autumn afternoon.
Above: Sun worshippers, Manly Cove.

Left: Summertime, Manly Beach.
Above: Locals, Shelly Beach.
Opposite page: Fishing North Harbour on a high tide.

activities

Opposite page : North Head cliffs at dawn.

Above & above right: Local fisherman, Travis Godfreyson with an Australia Salmon caught on his way to work.

Right: Acres of salmon boil in a feeding frenzy as Travis plays a fish off North Head.

Above: The Fat Lady has her annual refit at the Manly Cove Launch Club.

Opposite page: Malcom Kindred and Mark Williams work togther on their launch
Seascout on a Spring evening at the Manly Launch Club, founded in 1946.

WINCH OPERATION

WHEN OPERATING WINCH IN THE DOWN
POSITION MAKE SURE PAWL IS CLEAR
OF COG AT ALL TIMES. IF PAWL
BECOMES JAMMED RELEASE BY
OPERATING WINCH IN UPWARD POSITION
UNTIL PAWL IS FREE.

The swell is south easterly for days crashing heavily and clumsily along the coast and then a sudden and subtle change of wind direction, the surf is sublime....... a rising tide and a memorable afternoon for those able to catch the opportunity.

Optic fibre light sculpture by local installation artist
Warren Langley.

Left: 'Baskets', Manly Cove.

Opposite page: 'Trap', Collins Flat.

Above: British women tourists, Shelly Beach 1993.
Right: Travelling Man, 1993.

Above: These two beautiful girls were sitting on the beach all by themselves. They had come to Australia for one week and the day in Manly had to be spent on the beach even if the weather wasn't ideal, 1993

Opposite: Manly Wharf, the grand sea entrance to Manly.

Left: Kids busk during a competition at Manly Wharf.

community

Above: A special moment, Manly Wharf.

Left: Gospel Singer at the Manly Jazz Festival.

Left top: A wandering poet entertains young people at The Manly Wharf Bar.

Left centre: Clown busks on The Corso.

Opposite page: School girls prepare for their end of High School formal.

Above: Models at a charity fashion show, The International School for Hotel Management, St Patrick's Estate.

Right: 18th birthday party, North Steyne Surf Club.

Above: Bob Reid who lived for all his life with his sister Alice in their humble cottage in Balgowlah, 1992.

Above: Relaxed and comfortable before it was fashionable. These three regulars laughed their way though the days at Fairybower, 1993.

Left: Bush Artist Nick Petali with one of his art-works at Manly, 1993.

Middle: Old time boat men Manly Cove Launch Club, 1993.

Right: Man wearing his own home made jewellery waits in the beach shelter, South Steyne Manly, 1993.

Above: Surf School on Manly Beach.
Opposite page: Rodney Reynolds from Brewarrina in the surf.

Top left & above: Children play at East Esplanade.

Left: School kids head home at the end of day.

Opposite page: Schoolboy cricket under big Australian skies- Dobroyd Head

Opposite page: Manly Corso on a quiet night.
Above: A young guitarist busks, The Corso.

Left: The Corso, a place where buskers and street musicians can play and laugh.

Above: Manly born and bred Neil William. The long time resident believes that the suburb was settled by civilizations prior to Aboriginal.

Opposite page: 56 year old Peter James Fitzgerald sells the Big Issue at Manly Wharf. When he was 20 he earned $50,000 per year as a deep sea diver.

Opposite page : 78 year old Bruce Paterson cycles and swims winter and summer off Manly Beach.

Above: A beach sunbather of the old school, Vicky Hazelgrove has spent much of her 80 years enjoying the outdoor life on Australian beaches.

Opposite page: Proud father, John McSweeney gives away his beautiful daughter Susannah. Wedding held at St Patrick's Estate.

Above left: 18 mth old Sybella Macindoe expresses delight as she is led by her Aunt Elise to her first wedding at the Cerretti Chapel on Eastern Hill.

Above right: Wedding party.

Like many other small towns around Australia Manly remembers the dead on ANZAC day 25th March . As each year passes the parade changes. It is still a sombre occasion but these days there is room for kids and even the odd smile.

Left: ANZAC Day, 2007.
Opposite page: A family takes part in ANZAC memorial services held in The Corso.

history

At its core ANZAC day for Australians is primarily about remembering lost comrades but also about sadness and celebrating the terrible beauty of loss.

Above: Stone plaque signage of The Corso.

Opposite page: Ex- servicemen place bouquets of flowers in memory of dead comrades at The Corso War Memorial.

The Manly Quarantine Station is a poignant glimpse into Australia's past. There is a feeling of vastness and of a harsh colonial history in the architecture and its placement. Then below, the colour and life of the Sydney Harbour on a beautiful spring Sunday.

Above: A sculpture of Sir Edmund Barton Australia's first Prime Minister (1888-1893) overlooks Federation Point near Manly. The sculpture stands alongside one of Sir Henry Parkes who is known as the Father of Federation.

Opposite page: An early 18 footer sailing yacht, Manly Cove.

Left: This Edwardian inspired shelter is a special spot in Manly. Winter and summer it is used by an endless variety of friendly people. Perhaps the history or the open, see through architecture has some influence on the folk who sit there.

Opposite page: Heritage listed Manly Pier is what remains of the original pier, Manly Cove.

Above: Father and daughter at Fairy Bower in its perfect best. On days like this there is sense of ease and being that is hard to equal anywhere in the world.

Right: Women relax in their own worlds at Fairy Bower pool, Manly.

lifestyle

Above: Learning to surf with Dad, Queenscliff.

Above: Brazilian student Rodrigo Navajes contemplates on his first night in Manly. Navajes is one of thousands of Brazilians who has come to Manly to study in the past few years.

Above: Two surfers ride an afternoon wave at Queenscliff.
Right: The energy of youth.

Above: The Corso - the shopping, dining and entertainment hub of Manly.

Right: The Corso and the beach viewed from the Roof Bar of the Steyne Hotel.

Left: Sydneysiders share a drink on the Manly ferry as they go home from work in the harbour city.

Above: Manly Pier at Sunset.

Opposite page: Sydney skyline and Venus at last light.

The light and energy of the ocean affect people differently, some relax, some stretch hamstrings and others fall in love.

Opposite page: Tai Chi and relaxation, Dobroyd Head.

Above: Manly Ferry, couples and the Sydney Opera House.

Above: Looking out to the Sydney Heads on a winter's evening.

Above: A sheltered Manly Cove afternoon.

Above: Sunset colour at Ocean Beach.

Left: Big surf at Deadman's.

Opposite page: Beach bike, South Steyne Beach.

Above: Members of the Manly Surf club established in 1907 enjoy the gentle warmth of the winter sun, 1993.

Opposite page: South Steyne Beach shelter in 1993 before Council restoration.